Gardens of E

GARDENS of EDEN

Poems for Eve & Lilith

Michelene Wandor

JOURNEYMAN/PLAYBOOKS
London & New York

The Journeyman Press Limited, 97 Ferme Park Road,
Crouch End, London, N8 9SA and 17 Old Mill Road,
West Nyack, NY 10994, USA. Playbooks, c/o
Journeyman Press Ltd, London

Jointly published by the Journeyman Press and Playbooks,
1984

1 2 3 4 5 6 7 8 9 printing

ISBN 0 904526 92 5

The author would like to acknowledge that 'Eve in the
morning' has appeared in *New Departures*, and 'Eve at
Greenham Common' was performed as part of *Cut and
Thrust* cabaret, directed by Robyn Archer, at the Drill
Hall, London, 1983. 'A statue' appeared in the *PEN
Broadsheet*, Spring, 1984.

Printed in Great Britain

CONTENTS

Gardens of Eden

2   Eve, in the morning
4   Lilith, in the morning
5   Eve has a problem
5   Lilith and guilt
7   Eve and Lilith in a garden
8   Eve to Lilith
9   Lilith to Eve
10   Lilith finds a book
11   Lilith seeks a quest
12   Lilith chooses a quest
13   Eve gives counsel
14   Eve and Lilith make a pact
15   Ruth's story, as told to Lilith
16   Eve's commentary
17   Lilith in court
18   Eve's commentary
19   Lilith reads the proverbs
20   Eve has some gossip
20   Lilith's meditations
22   Lilith mourns with Nehemia, the man with a soul
23   Eve's commentary
24   Eve takes a trip
25   Lilith re-tells Esther's story
28   Eve visits Rome
29   Lilith comforts Job
31   Eve visits Greece: Persephone alone
32   Lilith on first love
33   Eve visits Greece: a statue
34   Eve meets Medusa
36   Lilith takes tea with the Lord
40   Eve comforts Lilith, from afar
41   Lilith faces the dark night of her soul

42 Eve visits Greece: Andromeda's turn
44 Lilith looks in the mirror
44 Eve, alone
45 Lilith looks ahead
47 Eve seeks refuge
49 Lilith dreams
49 Eve decides to return
50 Lilith thinks about loving
51 Eve wanders in another glade
52 Lilith's dance
54 Eve remembers birth
55 Lilith flies
56 Eve prepares: some invitations: dinner
60 Eve to Lilith
61 Lilith to Eve
61 Eve's poem

Other poems

65 letters to Virginia Woolf
67 on whether men can be feminists
68 Antigone 1
69 Antigone 2
70 Antigone 3
72 old man
73 argument
74 mapping gender, by the river
75 on visiting Sylvia Plath's grave
76 bingo
77 a bad dream
78 still life: man and woman at poetry reading
79 Eve visits the new cabaret, circa 1983
80 Eve at Greenham Common

And God said, Let us make man in our image, after our likeness . . . So God created man in his own image . . . male and female he created them. (*Genesis*, 26, 27)

After the Holy One created the first human being, Adam, He created a woman, also from the earth and called her 'Lilith'. Adam said: 'You are fit to be below me and I above you.' Lilith said: 'We are both equal because we both come from the earth.' (*Alphabet of Ben Sira*, 23 a–b)

And the Lord God caused a deep sleep to fall upon Adam and he slept; and he took one of his ribs and closed up the flesh instead thereof. And the rib, which the Lord God had taken from man, made he a woman, and brought her unto the man.
And Adam said, This is now bone of my bones and flesh of my flesh: she shall be called Woman, because she was taken out of Man. (*Genesis*, 21–23)

Eve, in the morning

So God created man (sic) in his (sic) own image?

'Male and female he created them'   Genesis 1:27

Look
it was only a tree, for God's sake
a nice tree
nice shade, green, leaves
an apple

You eat one apple and they remember you forever; you
only want to be left in peace, make
chutney, compote, dried apple rings
on a string

a snake? don't be silly
knowledge? you read too many Good Books
naked? so I like the sun. I tan easy.

Hava. Eve. Me

Sarah, Abraham's wife, the mother of Israel?
Well, let me tell you
you
couldn't tell
my chicken soup
from hers

you work your ribs to the bone
setting up the human race
and do you get any thanks?
a *nächtige tug* you get thanks
for freezing in
a goddam garden

2

I was glad we had to move, get
a decent place
those ants everywhere
and I mean everywhere

well, I've got a lot of grandchildren now
a little too much begetting, maybe
but as long as they've got their health and strength

I was always a good mother
no-one can say I wasn't
a good mother.

Lilith, in the morning

abstract art must truly be divine
for did not the Lord say

'thou shalt not make unto
thee any graven images or any likeness
of any thing that is in heaven above
or that is in the earth beneath
or that is in the water under the earth'   Exodus 20:4

gold and silver and brass

blue   purple   scarlet   linen
goat's hair
                oil for light   spices for anointing   oil
incense   onyx
                                emerald   sapphire
diamond   agate   amethyst

blue lace
                        bread and lamb

my burnt offerings
my tabernacle, my temple: art

myrrh   cinammon
olive oil

frankincense
                                stone tablets
pillars of cloud and fire

shining faces
almonds   flowers

oh God

4

Eve has a problem

what should I do?

the boys, Cain and Abel, they fight
fight, fight, all the time

what can you do?

I keep busy.

Lilith and guilt

a burnt offering, that's me
my blood sprinkled about
the altar of Adam's rib

no blood, no fat, thin and pale
I, the sacrificial lamb
flung out of heaven
because the Law
was made against me

when you are a burnt offering
you must atone and atone

for what sin? for what crime?

pillars of fire, salty, smoke
rancid
join the unclean, the hare
the camel the swine the prawn
the eagle the crab the raven
and the owl and the owl and the owl

touch me and you will go unclean
even unto my dead body
you may try to purify me, sprinkle my blood
at the foot of the altar
burn my sweet flesh for a sin offering
and still you will be unclean
you can never wash me away
I am the devil that haunts

I am neither cloven-hoofed
nor do I chew the cud

therefore you must break me, like an earthenware vessel

you may wash your clothes
till the fibres melt
into your skin, and still
you will be
unclean

for I
am the devil
that haunts

Eve and Lilith in a garden

cloud by day and fire by night
lungs clog damp by day
burn sharp by night
eyes will not close

no sleep

Mother Eve makes a fire, sweet
woodsmoking streaks breath
deep with smart freshness

Lilith changes the wind's direction
with a blink
clouds the sweetness with
acrid flashes, Eve
faces, eyes angry, Lilith signals
to her not to limit
the possibilities of fire
Lilith makes her cough, her eyes
look down, modest with pain

milk and honey stand curdled
and hard
between them

perhaps a stick with flowers on it
is needed
to prove healing?

perhaps a proper diet
might
do the trick

Eve to Lilith

don't get me wrong –
I have nothing against
first wives

ok, so you laid him
first; that's merely
a fact of life
so you got to know
all his little habits, like
picking his nose
when he reads in bed

he didn't do that with you?
I see

I'm not jealous. I don't
believe in jealousy, and
what I don't believe in
doesn't hurt me. But tell me
honestly, what did you do to the poor man?
He's a nervous wreck.
He can't stand up to his boss, he has
pains in his side all the time –
I mean, something must have happened
to leave a man
so scarred.

He's told me how beautiful you were.
The dark, dramatic type.

Usually he doesn't talk about you
but when we – well, long ago –
when – at night –
we – in the dark, always –
he used to call your name
at a certain moment.

It's none of my business
but you must have done
something very special
to make a man
remember you so

Lilith to Eve

I merely said 'no'.

That's when he gave me
his attention
for the first time

Lilith finds a book

Moses forty days and forty nights

forty years of some other hunger
in the wilderness
before I came upon
the Great Book, chapter
versed, marching columns deep
clenched each number, phase

I find laws:
two wives a man can have
kill a woman's parents, shave
her head, pare her nails
give her a month to mourn
and then fuck her: thus
the chosen tribe chooses

don't dress in each other's clothes

die if you are a virgin
die if you sleep with another man
die if you sleep with a woman
stone you if you are a whore

if he doesn't like you, he
can write his divorce down
and you may go

if your husband dies, his
brother can have you
keep it in the family

and still I see
                amethyst   agate

blue lace and spices
and Sarah, mother of Israel, smiling at me

but seven times round what city?
causing whose walls to fall?

Lilith seeks a quest

Deborah
here
judges Israel, a prophetess
under her tree

Jael hammers the nail into Sisera's temple
his head on the ground, now
forever doomed to listen
to the earth

Deborah sings, to see
such fun
and she hugs Jael

Oh, I am bitter for my sin of simple being

I would not be a priest for anything

when I bleed my flowers be upon me or my man
he is unclean
when I bear
I am unclean
when I take his seed into me
I am unclean
I must atone and separate from my uncleanness
I must not eat blood
for it is the life of all flesh
he must not see me naked, for I am his
nakedness

if blood and life and nakedness
cannot meet in one flesh, where
is holiness?

there is something unfinished
that is holy, a grape in the corner
of the vineyard, for the poor to eat

*it is hard to love my neighbour
as myself*

Lilith chooses a quest

women fight, women prophesy, women
lead, women judge

when Samson is born
Delilah becomes the betrayer of strength
Deborah is delighted

Eve gives counsel

Jael,
why don't you take up a hobby?
I hear carpentry's very
popular with girls nowadays.

Delilah, hairdressing would suit
you. A little skill with the scissors
would do no harm.

Deborah, for God's sake
stop
all that giggling.

Eve and Lilith make a pact

Eve: What are we fighting over?

Lilith: I don't know.

Eve: Is it a man?

Lilith: Is it a book?

Eve: It might be a man.

Lilith: I don't think so.

Eve: Is it a garden?

Lilith: Perhaps so.

Eve: Perhaps it's the world.

Lilith: I don't know.

Eve: If we don't know,
         we'd better look.
         I'll take the world.

Lilith: I'll take the book.

Eve: Come on. I'll show you around.

Ruth's story, as told to Lilith

She was left with two sons.
Then they too died and we, their wives, strangers
to her blood, remained: Orpah and I, Ruth. My name
like anger, my temperament to match: passion
it would be called, if
roused to love or fury.

I don't know why I loved her;
simply to follow
Naomi was all I desired.
I even rose to the heights
of poetry: 'Whither thou goest,' I said,
'I will go; where thou lodgest, I will lodge,
thy people shall be my people
and thy God my God.
Where thou diest, will I die
and there will I be buried.'

Not so much did I promise her son
in my heart, my husband.

I have been a stranger
all my life.

We returned to Bethlehem
with the barley harvest, Naomi
calling herself Mara, she who is
bitter.

For bread I gleaned
corn in Boaz' field, dusted
golden sheaves in the setting sun.

Well, one thing leads to another
and Naomi's husband's land
passed to the hand
of Boaz, and I with it.
Such is the scythe that comes between women.

Naomi dances my child now, and
the line continues. Sheaves smile
in her iris eyes when she looks at me. They say I am
better to her than
seven sons had been. They do not
know how much I love her, more
than I could seven sons.

I am still a stranger.

Eve's commentary

Ruthie, I'd like
to give you the benefit
of my advice:

you should never get too
involved
with a mother-in-law.

Lilith in court

two harlots, they were
(what you and I would now call
two single mothers)
                        the two alone one night (as usual)
one baby died
its mother swapped it with the living
and Solomon in his supposed wisdom
forced the truth into the open
(apparently)

as though the dead child's mother
would have time for anything
but howling grief, as though
another's child
could replace the cooling warmth in her heart

Lilith knows: I have had
many children and sent them
all forth to people the air

in court
the mothers laughed
in Solomon's face, to see a man
suppose that any woman's grief
could so craze her
that she would see
another child
put to death

a mother becomes a jealous god to
avenge her child
not to destroy for the sake
of an act of will, let alone
for a cheap moral ending

Eve's commentary

be fair: you're
taking it all a
little bit
too literally

what about Solomon's proverbs?
there's an achievement

Lilith reads the proverbs

three thousand proverbs
and songs one thousand and five, beneath
whose shade I may dream:

cedar trees
            from Lebanon   fir trees

a temple of wood, warm cedar
and gold   olive trees
                            hard wood

seven years

two hundred pomegranates
                        lilies

lions   oxen   cherubim

gold candlesticks
            hinges of gold

the glory of the Lord comes on a gold cloud

followed by plagues, pestilences and locusts

Eve has some gossip

They say
Jezebel slew the prophets.

It's rubbish.
She was with me all the time.

Lilith's meditations

One

fire comes down from heaven
and consumes men – just
like that

how many miracles can a woman do?
give birth
bleed
love

and with all these miracles
still seem
unclean

what more must she do?
conjure up chariots of fire? horses of fire?

should she smite the waters, that they
might part (*pace* Elijah)?

turn children into bears?

no

obey   obey   obey

this is her impossible miracle

Jezebel, eaten by dogs
for doing nothing
that I can fathom
merely what she was told

only her skull
her feet
and the palms of her hands left
all the better to see you with
sockets follow you
bloody hands touch you
her blood sprinkled on your bread

someone has bad dreams

Two

the miracles are the best
columns of fire and salt and cloud
even a plague from nowhere
fills dying nostrils
with sweet incense

there is no peace in the Old Testament
all rush and worry, worry and rush

a broken Bible poises
my palm, my left
palm, whole and warm

a house filled with a cloud

Lilith mourns with Nehemia, the man with a soul

what with smiting and weeping
and fasting and mourning
and plagues and diseases

and sinning and corrupting and
sinning
and corrupting
and sackcloth
and seed
and all that begetting
and the smell
and burnt offerings

enough to make anyone
welcome
Jesus and penicillin
with open arms, eh?

Eve takes a trip

the soup's on a low flame
clean socks and shirts
in the cupboard

I breathed polish on the candlesticks
I dusted the incense

butter's in the freezer
chopped liver in the
pottery dish covered with cling-film

all you need to buy
each day
is bread and fruit

the biscuit tin is full
and there's a new
packet of matza
on the top shelf

I'm taking some ham
and pickle sandwiches
on rye

expect me when you see me

Lilith re-tells Esther's story

the world rustles for Esther
in her best red weave

only nine chapters, she has
little time to coin a magic mine

meanwhile, back at the palace, King Ahasuerus
feasts the men, while meanwhile
behind the palace, Queen Vashti
feasts the women.

Vashti is summoned to the king's presence
but being rosy with the jokes
of women, she puts her foot down

fuck off, you wally (or some Old Testament
equivalent), I won't be shown off like
a prize cow this time

the lads, of course, don't take to that at all
because everyone knows that once a queen
sets a bad eg
any woman could take it into her
head to disobey
her lord and master

get rid of Vashti, advise
the princes, fear seaming their pores,
replace her with another – after all,
every man
should bear rule
in his own house

so King A orders a load
of virgins (what's so special
about virgins?) from whom
to choose a replacement
for Vashti

meanwhile, back in the ghetto
Mordecai, the Jew, hears of this and sends
his cousin Hadassah (Esther to you)
along with the other virgins, and lo,
she is chosen with a select few
for further tests (the king conveniently
unaware of her ethnic origins)

a year of 'purification'; oil of
myrrh, sweet odours, and one by one,
in turn, in turn, the young women
are set before the king
for him to try
till he gets bored

Esther, however, does not bore him
at all, and as her reward, King A
sets the crown upon her head
and her body in his bed

Mordecai meanwhile hovers round the gate

also meanwhile, a bad man
called Haman
becomes King A's right-hand man,
a misnomer for such a sinister man
who likes all
to bow down
before him

Mordecai, always a meanwhile man,
refuses to bow, and in revenge Haman
decides to kill all
the Jews (where
have we heard that one since?)

anyway, the long and the short of it is that
Esther so continues to please King A
with her courage and her beauty
that Haman is sussed out
and hanged
the Jews are saved
and Mordecai rises
to be second-in-command
to King A

there is something missing
from this story:
someone
somewhere
doesn't bother to say
whether Esther
actually liked
King A

Eve visits Rome

Pope Joan

A lady pope?

Who gets pregnant?

Do me a favour.

Lilith comforts Job

poor Job
you did try

but finally you freaked and cursed
as would anyone whose sheep
were burned, whose body was covered
in boils

you did not, of course,
know of the bet
God and Satan were
waging over your soul

you tried saying 'the Lord
giveth and the Lord taketh away
blessed be the Lord'
but there came a point
where it just
didn't sound right

all you wanted was justice
a fair fight
God to face you face to face
not simply strike
from behind a cloud

no-one likes a moody man
no-one likes another's anger

they came from all sides
telling you to pray
to keep your good counsel
to believe   to believe   to believe
but you stuck to your guns
could not cease questioning
would not abandon your integrity

you asked for help for them that
have no power, for
those with no strength to be saved
for if God was truly with you, you argued,
then God would cast you out if you pretended to
be other than you were

'the price of wisdom is above rubies,' you said
Job 28:18

but of course
in the end
after the Lord
has spent chapters challenging you
to a competition
of creation and power

of course you repented

who can compete with a man
who creates a world
in seven days?

Eve visits Greece

One: Persephone alone

like a
finger-tip gliding over
ivory, I
smooth my evening

once more in harmony, I sit
among familiars: white
daisies under my hands, my
curtain of swinging hair a
band of lace

here I can remember
that the seventh note
is always sharp; the seventh
month the time of my leaving,
the seventh day a small plateau
of rest

here I am invisible
no mother
no dark lord
here I spike stars
on my knuckles
kick rainbows
like dry leaves in autumn

here I stitch my plans
and knit
my revolution

here, in the house of anonymity
I love myself
I am defiant as cactus
I am unnamed, per se,
Persephone peeled pitted
towards an obligation
she chooses

Lilith on first love

            well, you were
my evil eye, you
came along with your
on-the-road mentality
you were
a play with name unspeakable
you
beckoned me, an innocent
to superstition's grip

a drum, a drum beat
my heart wild, no witch's
cauldron could draw me
from your corporeal eye
no ritual exorcism
keep me from
your name dreamed,
a real man
with no need to beckon
me on, just the being
enough.
            Lilith, you
called me. I, your name,
never spoke

Eve visits Greece

Two: a statue

head   red   fronds

friends, they might have –
                              a red flag

feast his eyes, he could not:
a stone, his head, perhaps
his eyes black pips, spat
out by the snakes, her hair

only wings on his heels, not
his mind

Perseus, Medusa;
lovers they might have been
but when he looked at her
he thought he saw
snakes where her hair

she, pinned below him,
reaches
to caress his leg
feels wings at his ankle flutter
with fear

her marble breast beats
below his foot
his sword shielding his guilt

a moment, and
her neck cracks
green and white marble melon
in the square, water
marble   melon

pink shy outer layer, fury
passion-tongued, squirms
in his hand, foams over her
rose heart

Eve meets Medusa

Medusa. Sit down. Take
the weight off your snakes. We have
a lot in common. Snakes, I mean.

Tell me, can you really turn men
to stone with a look? Do you
think, if I had a perm –
maybe not.

Don't you think
Perseus was
a bit of a coward? not even
to look you in the face

you were beautiful when you
were a moon goddess, before
Athene changed your looks
through jealousy

I can't see what's wrong
with making love
in a temple, even
if it was her temple

it's a good mask; you must
feel safe and loving
behind it

you must feel very powerful

tell me, what conditioner do you use?

Lilith takes tea with the Lord

One

'the Lord knoweth the way
of the righteous
but the way of the ungodly
shall perish'   Psalms 1:16

how do you recognise an enemy?
leave it to the Lord: he knows

but I cannot act out of someone
else's knowledge

tell me, why
should you have a monopoly
on anger and rage, revenge
and punishment

what about me

ok, so you made heaven and earth
and the stars   so?
no-one
asked you, did I ask you, I wasn't even made, how
could I ask you?

anyway, you're only interested in man (sic)
you put all things under his feet, including women
and still you expect gratitude

let me tell you, Lord,
your characters are taking over

you will fall into the ditch you are digging

I searched for a joyful psalm, to let me
praise and praise
instead I am beginning to feel
crabby again, oh Lord
why do I bother

what about us being nice
to each other?

you fly upon the wings of the wind
you hail stones and coals of fire
you shoot arrows of lightning
and the breath from your nostrils
burns

you have all the good bits
and I scare easy

Two

you are as a bridegroom
coming out of your chamber, rejoicing as a
strong man to run a race

ever macho, eh, Lord

there's a thing I'd like
to say
I am not happy when I am afraid
and if I am simply to fear you, then
I must be unhappy, right?
what pleasure do you get
from unhappy people?
what *nachas*?

remember when you said, 'fight
against them that fight against me'
that struck a chord:
                          for if they that without cause
have hid for me their net in a pit,
then shall their net that they have hid
catch themselves unawares, then indeed
my soul will be joyful and rejoice
in your salvation

I want to be my own jealous God, you see

for the irony is,
I am made only too well
in thine image, the
image of a jealous God (see Psalm 35)

'the meek shall inherit the earth'?
I have not learned meekness from watching you

you have made me
the heathen in my own heart
I have invaded myself
I am a stranger in my midst
I do not belong
to myself

I dream that the
wings of a dove might suit me
soft, loving peace calling
unto me, and I could fly away, far

but your tongue is a sharp sword
your teeth spears
and my heart a snapped string

you give me yourself with one hand
and with the other
you take me away
how the hell do I know
where the hell
I am

I could play music for you
I could sing my poems for you
I could make you laugh
I could learn to make soup, knit
a coat of many colours for you

but I will not sit in sackcloth
will not dry my palms with ashes
will not eat the dust
for that does not celebrate you
and that does not celebrate me
and I am into fairness
which means we must both
get enough out of it
a little word
reciprocity

you say you will hover over me
your wings
giving me protection
I've got news for you
I'm allergic to feathers

Three

yes, you did do some nice things
silver and gold, water and fire
bread and quails
and *matza brei*

must have been a lot of work
proof-reading the tablets
(keep taking the tablets,
I hear myself think;
sorry, Lord)

I did sit down by the
waters of Babylon
and wept
Oh, I wept so much

when I sat down it
was a gentle flow
and when I got up
after weeping
there they were,
the waters of Babylon
my waters
my tears that made a stream
a river

a sea

Eve comforts Lilith, from afar

'every wise woman buildeth her house'   Proverbs 14:1

excuse me, Lord
I have to take delivery
of some bricks

a dry person, broken
into many selves

I am rigid with
the fear of dust

a dry person, a
woman who hacks girders
against green hillsides
stacking old moments
on an open palm

she hears through stone walls
she craves you
she shells your skull hollow
on the outside
you need not go far
to think, she surprises you
she is stainless, hurt
brushes off her

a dry person
rinses you away
a solid swirling mist
into a dark nowhere
a dry person
always sees the sky
a dry person
darkens the ground
at your feet, rocks
your shape
the dry woman turns
ash, stings
your instep, clings
under your eyelids

you cannot lean into the hill
for the dry woman will stone you
lean into the valley
she will push you

she is a hollow wind
jumping at your back
she tries to shield from you
your knowledge
that you must grow
where you fall

Eve visits Greece

Three: Andromeda's turn

Perseus is a tomorrow
sort of person, dashing fresh
from killing an unseen
Medusa to
save Andromeda

hell is yesterday's pit, fixed in fear
of someone who once helped her
to do good –
a monster good at fixing
a lavatory cistern, and she knew
she wasn't bothered by looks as such:
the 'monster' was a man who listened

Andromeda now, a peach stone
against rock's flesh
wrists rasp and back skins
against a cliff
which everyone fears (hence ideal
for sacrifice, thinks the village)

an angry sea, grey with hunger
no fish in its belly
for months
no bread
for days
so a quick-fathomed decision
was taken
based on the waves
in her hair, amber waves
to taunt the raging grey

they grabbed her in the middle
of a cup of nectar, peach juice
staining her chin, can't
reach to lick it up, won't let
her use the back of her hand

when she was a child
Andromeda dreamed
of gracing a powerful man, handsome,
feared by everyone, godlike, even;

now she curses her misunderstood arrogance
and waits for the winged beauty
to save her from
her one chance of heaven

Lilith looks in the mirror

my skin is silk, my tongue is wine
my teeth are sunlight
my nails are fine linen

when I walk
I sail like a ship
in a fresh wind

I am beautiful
and need not be told so

I belong to no-one
and my own works
praise me in the gates

the word 'virtue' is not
in my vocabulary
'strength' is

Eve, alone

when you're tired
you cry

the sky has been tired
for days

Lilith looks ahead

'there is no new thing under the sun'   Ecclesiastes 1:9

you may have to
cloud your sun
for what I say
is new

to every thing there is a season
and a time
to every purpose
under the heaven
a time to be born
and a time to die
a time to plant
and a time to pluck up that which is planted
a time to kill
and a time to heal

a time to weep and a time to laugh
a time to mourn
and a time to dance

a time to embrace
and a time
to refrain from embracing

a time to get
and a time to lose
a time to keep
and a time to cast away
a time to rend
and a time to sew
a time to keep silence
and a time to speak

a time to love
and a time to hate
a time of war
and a time of peace

best is the sight of the eyes
and the wandering of desire

and then who dares say
that sorrow is better than laughing

for now there is a thing
that's new, a thing
that brings
its own season

not only man is wise
not only woman the ensnarer

evil, madness and death:
them will I live among
but by them be not touched

if I eat my bread with joy
and my wine with a merry heart
it is because I
have seen happiness, have heard
joy and know what
I have seen and heard

my eyes are not vanity
my ears are not vanity
my skin is not vanity

I will not fear
that which I cannot see
that which I cannot hear

I will even welcome bad dreams

Eve seeks refuge

my feet are killing me; rope
sandals and leaf mulch don't mix
and a forest is a hard
path when you're not as fit
as you were

a hut   suspended in the air

stilts? tripods? magic?
feet   legs   chicken legs
three chicken legs. A hut
on three chicken legs.

a door – open
a fire – burning
yeast, a hot loaf, crusty from the oven
tea   a samovar steaming
a chair   cushions

paradise; this is the garden of Eden

Baba Yaga flies above me,
rows her way through clouds
sweeps her flight path away
with her broom, besom-brisk, soars
and swoops and sweeps and sways
and when she's lonely her
chicken legs run her home
to another part of the forest

Baba, never bored, ever busy

Baba – buba – someone lost,
something heavy, a heavy
wanting – a mother – and who
was Eve's mother?

a mother who sweeps trouble
away, wipes tears, is always
there, in spirit if not in apron

Baba flies
Baba twists
Baba has no house of gingerbread
but a sturdy shelter
Baba is not evil
but powerful
Baba waves and flies

Baba has a meal set out for me
a bed warming for me
a loom weaving for me
porridge just right for me
Baba writes a book for me
paints pictures on my eyelids
warms my hands in hers

Baba touches me gently
on the shoulder
tells me
it's time
to move on

Lilith dreams

the Lord rocks me to sleep
makes sure I have his dreams
and then protests
when I wake
from a nightmare

Eve decides to return

There's something about
the quiet of your own front door
that makes it musical
after absence

Lilith thinks about loving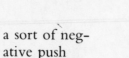

a sort of neg-
ative push   the valley
spins cupidity

I lie, sucking earth,
stones gravel my lips
granite strokes my cheek

I have been sour, eaten
with hate, I admit it
I have no more shame

the ground has spat me
forth, frothed me
at its corners

I curl and hammer
flat my hands   palm splat blades
green my fingers

seeping a late dew softens me
my hand on my face
I might learn to forgive

Eve wanders in another glade

here
a Narcissus
who traded in his manhood
in order to spend all day
recognising himself

here
Peter Pan
who traded in his manhood
in order to avoid
recognising himself

neither grew up

on the edge of the pool
Echo shivers with guilt: all
she did was show him
(Narcissus)
she loved him
by giving him back his words

by the front door
Wendy stands
puzzled
all she did was show him
(Peter Pan)
how much she loved him
by warming his slippers

Adam, does any of this
ring a bell?

Lilith's dance

Lilith sins?

Lilith sings
Lilith speaks many a cross word
Lilith has an anger like love
like a procession of pillars
of fire
Lilith has the delight
of a woman scorned

he modelled me
I was his clay thing
into me he breathed life
I became his *golem*
I went forth and I destroyed
havoc my middle name

I am the *dybbuk* of delight
I slip into the souls
of those who need me

perhaps you breathed
just a little
too much life, a sniffle too long
but once tasting the air
I would not be still, not
be silent, not return
to my feet of clay

I will not gather dust
I do not cower beneath cobwebs
I do not fear the hot streets
I walk
in the middle
of the pavement

I do not hug the shade
of cowardly buildings
I do not stay in my ghetto
but I strut and stride
into the ghetto
of men
I interrupt
the invisible universal
which denies men their souls
and women their being

I do not creep

I do not crawl

see

I am proud

I have taken the cloth
from my mirror
of mourning

for your birthday
(if gods have birthdays)
I shall give you
a mirror

Eve remembers birth

the first stage

looking skywards
night dusts
eyes shell light
dark husks darkness

the second stage

the ship has rocked silently
now sense the wind waving
someone billows
translucence
at night havens hum, a slow, soft
ticking, lazy between
curling surf

the third stage

the whale in the womb
finger-thrusts starwise out
nudge-noses soft horizons
glistens and dances
grows and softens
sleeks a path
to a cold, edgy awakening
and the discovery
of a warm love
that begins to
compensate

Lilith flies

glass night protects
you, flying high
above
pestilences and plagues:

from a great height
blood shines, and
locusts carve poems
out of clouds

your children fly round
you, their wings cooling
and warming by turns, they
breathe fire and salt

their shining faces
are spice and song

you smile

Eve prepares

I have passed over from
my Egypt
into the world
I have eaten the bread of strangers
who became friends

I have slept in the houses
of others, and listened
to decisions
that became mine

I have found that my world
can sit on my back, a cross
between Atlas and a snail,
the strength of both
and the delicacy
of both

I have found that sleep can come
anywhere
that warmth can be built
that the world is larger than one garden

I am preparing, therefore,
the first dinner
to which I shall invite
the family of my choice

the forest gave me a tree, with thick strong
green needles
when I carried it across
my threshold, the sharp greenness
turned shimmer-silver, a thousand
shadows in light, slim and flat, a
transparent tree which shines shadow
into winter light

some invitations

Jael is carving me a large table

Deborah has promised not to pass judgement
on the dinner, unless it's praise

Delilah is planning to dye her
hair green, to go
with the new curtains
and the tree

Ruth and Naomi are bringing
a double sleeping-bag

Pope Joan can leave the baby
in my bedroom; Solomon's
two lady friends are bringing
their babies too
Perseus and Peter Pan will
amuse the children with flying tricks

the Queen of Sheba is dropping
in after dinner
for a cognac

Jezebel can leave the dogs outside

Esther and Vashti will bring the
book they are writing together, and
doubtless argue all the way
through dinner

Persephone is bringing her mother;
they can sit opposite one another

Medusa and her Gorgon sisters
are going to play a trio for recorders

Andromeda is bringing some seaweed,
chinese-style-fried

Baba Yaga and Sarah are both
bringing chicken soup

Wendy is just going
to enjoy herself
for a change

and that nice girl Judy, from
Chicago, who is very fond of
dinner parties,
is coming

that's a lot of guests; a lot
of *kneidlach*

the dinner

I am lighting candles in memory
because they give a beautiful light
and a candle will always
look you in the eye, straight

a candle gives you many pictures

ritual is a good thing
everything in order, everything
ordered, a Seder, an order
to events, courses of action
and an order for eating

here, of course, is the empty
place, the space for
the uninvited guest, a prophet,
a strange Elijah, a dark,
vibrant woman
to drink a cup of sweet red wine
a silver cup for her, a cup
with no stem, no handle
to be clasped between both hands, a goblet
of sparkling hope

the absent friend,
awaited

Eve to Lilith

your mouth is a pomegranate
ripening in smile

I can see into the garden
my sister, my love

I have mixed you a banana milk shake
milk to make your bones strong
banana to make the adrenalin
course through your blood

your throat is a white pillar
I stand and watch you drink
I am swimming into your heart
your cheeks are a bed of spices
your eyes are bay leaves
your legs are pillars of marble

you are too thin
come into my kitchen

Lilith to Eve

you hide your face
let me touch you
your skin is soft as peaches
your hand a gentle lily

your shoulders are the slopes
of Lebanon
your arms the strong cedars
the mist of your breath
is home

you are blue lace
and spices

Eve's poem

We must go in.
The others are waiting.

OTHER POEMS

letters to Virginia Woolf

My dear Virginia,
How dare I admit that I
have not enjoyed reading
your novels – indeed,
that I have never finished any of your novels,
except the love of my life, Orlando?

Dear Virginia,
I have read and re-read 'A Room of One's Own'
(although I no longer quote from it
with the pride of fresh discovery
because these days absolutely every other
feminist in the world quotes from it . . .)
and I must say
I like your style, I really do, your elegant
teasing sentences
floating like a diver's lifeline.

Dear Virginia,
Why don't I like the same detachment
in your novels (except, of course,
for the wondrous Orlando)?

Dear Virginia,
I bet you would hate to meet me.

Dear Virginia,
You remind me of a friend I once had,
long large hands held
out; a fire, gas,
burned blue and pink, a late
conversation, God and art,
entwined us, she folded

on a patch of
worn Persian carpet, her
hair sleek, wound heavy over
her ears. She was a kind of sister
before I understood a new meaning
for the word.

Dear Virginia,
You made your own family,
from Orlando to Vita – such discreet choices –
plus a gentleman in America whose
address you lost,
the officials of the British Museum,
and Orlando of the soft eyes and misty plumes,
and Orlando who had sixteenth-century lusts
and Orlando whose pages crumble between my fingers

Dear Virginia,
I dream of my own Orlando.
My Orlando stretches, yawns and rides
to her love in any century,
the dampness of desire haloes her breath
her bones are made of frost and melt
in the heat of warm, dark ink.
My Orlando skates feather pictures with her toes,
joins my hands with hers
in her fur tippet, swings and swirls
and beckons and beckons.

Dear Virginia,
I will try Mrs Dalloway again.
I promise.

on whether men can be feminists

if it is true
that women
have no sense of humour
(we can't tell a joke,
can't remember funny stories,
not like a witty bloke)

and if it is true
that feminists
of all women
especially
and particularly
have no sense of humour

then it must follow
from that –
assuming that God
gave all the wit to men –
it must follow
irrevocably
and incontrovertibly
that men
cannot
be feminists

QED

Antigone 1

Antigone with Oedipus
another kind of Cordelia
to another kind of Lear

she sees the city for him
she softens the rock with her voice
she, no stranger to devotion

she guides, Oedipus makes the speeches

Antigone, a good girl since womanhood
did not sit meekly at home to sew
but chose the wild, to sew
comfort for blind Oedipus

Ismene, her sister, remained within four walls
to sew
it is she who brings news of their
brothers' strife

Polynices banished and Eteocles
(who always grabbed the best grapes)
stayed within the walls of Thebes

Antigone has her hands full, what with
a fire for night, water
to wash Oedipus' wounds, air
to plan for the day

she pleads that Oedipus speak
to Polynices, the family that ties together
flies together
she rushes between father and son, oh yes, noble, oh yes, brave

and yet   and yet

my daughters have been loyal to me,
says Oedipus; they
are my sons

Antigone pleads with Polynices
to turn his army back – why fight your brother? what mess
of pottage is at stake

she knows that it is spelled pride, that
faces fall and are lost in such battles
Antigone has always loved Polynices' face, the full
lips that laugh so easily, the lion's
profile, the confident thighs

Antigone is being uneconomical: asking
a lot of questions and
getting no answers

no-one asks her anything

Antigone 2

Only Theseus saw Oedipus die; his
daughters ('sons'?) barred
from watching
only women, after all

Theseus is king
                women weep; and they do

Antigone cannot bear her loss
and wishes to die also

Ismene thinks about the next meal

Theseus will return the daughters
to Thebes

Theseus is king

Antigone 3

Antigone, twice bereft

Polynices dead, decreed
naked, decreed undignified,
decreed open to the sky

first, some dust
on his corpse, naked, pink
and purple; remembered the sweetness
that came forth from
the lion
somewhere else
and wept for Polynices' smile
and lack of fur
he, the lion in steel and iron
nearly no threat in life, not really,
not to one who knew him,
still a threat in death

her hand fears rotting and the vultures
take their time

Creon punishes the living
by not allowing
the dead to hide
their shame

never a moment of doubt, Antigone
always a woman
who put her family
first

here, again, she has something to do

a second time she digs deeper
her hands furrow a bed
the crumbling earth like loose linen
the stones for a blanket
careless in their pillowing fall

I offered three times to the dead
I screamed
there must be time to mourn
you do not understand
I do it for myself, not
for him and honour, that
I may cover my sorrow

old man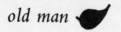

grabbing   in crisis

all your life you have lived
with rage

now a tear topples hatred, you become
a Samson fighting against
the scissors

somewhere an error of communication, wires
which never crossed, someone
forgot to touch wire ends

now you must mourn alone
black earth soiled your heart
sticky with bully's blood
steel sliced your semi-detached castle
away from the love of vellum
my illuminated letters just so much
compost, shivering brown in your stare

your misery
like a scorched ditch
after harvest

argument

warm the bricks
peep hard through
the hard glass
oblong gaze through
the Venetian blinds
slat yourself
against the warm brick
rub your back, arch
your fair mind

I am still looking for you
looking out through
my hard black window
my share of the language
piling up around me

mapping gender, by the river

I tried a compass
        got vertigo

I follow the signs
        the crow flies above me

no-one looks at me along the rocks

I stripe and square the hill
            I think of putting my hand

along the valley
        sideways
            the outside edge of my hand

I can't ignore the mill chimney
            no longer used

I think of taking my other hand
            and running it cupped
down the bricks
        I would prefer lying in the grass, myself

to being so alone and exposed

if I occupy both hands thus

I will be stuck in this valley for ever

so I wipe my hands
        against my legs

and I walk free
        into the town

on visiting Sylvia Plath's grave

a spike of trees
handling
breath

perhaps she
ran into a
woolgatherer
who fleeced her
coatless

her mind picked
out in coarse fluff
caught on twigs

the wind hollowing at
her back
urging her on

the poet's wife
(I mean, of course, the poet)
who committed suicide
and whose words
found comfort
where she
could not

choking a rose
leaves red lines
on your palm

a moment of roulette
no excitement
just a dull, aching pull
downward

bingo

woos
　　forgets

sees
　　vets
spaces out his
　　　　　her
says doubt made
pain faulty
ought to
get better
　　　why not?

too bald, that
　　　　　age takes the
children
　　　continue

no new words
even forget a few
the stages are dreaded
and alternatives are worse

until at the end
only a walk in the snow
is possible
　　　tough

not even a fleck of concrete
to tie the
moments welded

see you soon, they
all say
woos tomorrow
for seeing you yesterday

forgotten won't bring it back
                                        better luck
                                        next time

a bad dream

leaves couldn't care less
scorn hollies
in my ear
alien eyes catch
me in passing
hook a glance
on the way in
everything falls, falling
a seagull scavenging
for fulfilment
pecking at my feet

still life: man and woman at poetry reading

the woman poet
up on the platform
with the man poet
smiles up at him
when he introduces himself
(she is seated and he
stands)

he begins by handing his compliment
to the fair sex: someone,
he says, once said that since
God gave so much power to woman,
there was absolutely no need at all
to gild the lily
by giving her the vote too

the woman poet smiles up at him
it could be that she has not heard
it could be that she really
thinks it's witty, since she did
earlier reassure the audience that a)
she was not angry about the
Bomb, just sad, and b) that
she had once been attacked
at a reading by
'a group of feminists'
for one of her poems

the man poet
then reads
a poem about puberty; words like
'loins' and 'tree'
and 'imagination' appear
to be important

the woman poet is still smiling
it could be that she
needs all the protection she can wear
it could be that we
need all the protection we can muster

some of the women poets
not on the platform
leave at the interval

Eve visits the new cabaret, circa 1983

These new poets
they rhyme
they scan

why did we fight World War II
if not to

free verse

Eve at Greenham Common

I can see from here
it's a little messy

the grass is much blacker
on the other side

one day I will tell you
of my garden

such a beautiful garden
such a healthy
garden

a garden where the balance
of ethical behaviour
is as perfect
as convolvulus
and cucumber

and lest you think
my garden is mere
bourgeois idealism, let
me tell you, the
atmosphere was such
that even the occasional enmity.
between ladybird
and aphid
could be tolerated

I can see your garden, a desert
flowered
with webs of bright wool

one day I will tell you of my garden

and of the day when the mushrooms
arrived in damp triumph
and bred among
themselves
some toadstools

and the air was filled with a word
and that word
was
ownership

I can see your garden, daisy-chained
with hands of all shapes
and sizes

one day I)will tell you
of my garden
a dialectical paradise, such a
blooming of thesis, antithesis
and synthesis as to make the
balance of nature
look like an egg-timer
in simplicity

such a bouquet
of beautiful
contradictions

now I will tell you
a story
how some women choose
and how some
(like your lady Thatcher) choose
even to be Tories
and write stories
with unhappy endings

she had a little mushroom
nothing would it bear

remember my friend, Medusa?
a powerful woman
but powerful at some cost
a woman you couldn't look
in the eye
for fear
she might turn you
to stone
a woman with snakes for hair
a woman who could sting
with a look

right now
Medusa is at the
hairdressers
trying to decide
whether to keep her strength
but let her power flow
in some better direction, without
her snaky locks

she must make her choice
for herself

this spring I plan
to weed out the fungus
and plant African violets
deep and purple

one day you must visit
my garden